AQUATIC

HACKS

FOR

MINECRAFTERS

AN **UNOFFICIAL**
MINECRAFTERS GUIDE

HACKS

FOR

MINECRAFTERS

THE UNOFFICIAL GUIDE TO TIPS AND TRICKS THAT OTHER GUIDES WON'T TEACH YOU

AQUATIC

MEGAN MILLER

Sky Pony Press
New York

Sky Pony Press books may be purchased in bulk at special discounts for sales promotion, corporate gifts, fund-raising, or educational purposes. Special editions can also be created to specifications. For details, contact the Special Sales Department, Sky Pony Press, 307 West 36th Street, 11th Floor, New York, NY 10018 or info@skyhorsepublishing.com.

Sky Pony® is a registered trademark of Skyhorse Publishing, Inc.®, a Delaware corporation.

Minecraft® is a registered trademark of Notch Development AB.
The Minecraft game is copyright © Mojang AB.

Visit our website at www.skyponypress.com.

10 9 8 7 6 5 4 3 2 1

Library of Congress Cataloging-in- Publication Data is available on file.

Series design by Brian Peterson
Interior screenshots by Megan Miller

Print ISBN: 978-1-5107-6193-3
Ebook ISBN: 978-1-5107-6521-4

Printed in China

TABLE OF CONTENTS

This guide is based on the 1.15.2 version of the Minecraft Java Edition, so some features may have changed, or been added or removed between writing this book and publication. There are some minor differences between the Java Edition and the Bedrock Editions of Minecraft, although these tend to be minimal and are reconciled as development of the editions for the two platforms continue.

CHAPTER 1

THE AQUATIC BIOMES OF MINECRAFT

The biomes of Minecraft are the different natural environments you find, like desert or forest. There used to be only one type of ocean in Minecraft, and it was pretty barren, but today there are lots of different aquatic environment with their own unique features. In Minecraft, biomes are given different sky colors (sometimes), leaf and grass colors, as well as different plants and mobs that can spawn there. Different Minecraft ocean biomes will have different water colors, ocean beds, structures, and flora (plants) and fauna (animals).

The ocean biomes have different shades of blue for their water and temperatures associated with each shade. From left to right are the water colors of the Warm Oceans, Lukewarm Oceans, Oceans, Cold Oceans, and Frozen Oceans.

What's Aquatic?
Aquatic means "watery" or "waterlike", and it comes from the Latin word for water, "aqua." Aquatic biomes in the real world are environments that are in water, from marine biomes (oceanic biomes) to freshwater biomes like lakes, rivers, and wetlands.

Ocean

The original aquatic biomes in Minecraft is the Ocean biome and it counts for the greatest amount of Overworld area in any normal world – over a quarter of any world will be Ocean. If you include all ocean biomes, a Minecraft world will be over half ocean. Sea level (the top of the ocean) in Minecraft is at y=63, and an ordinary ocean's floor is around y=48. Oceans typically have gravelly floors (with some exposed stone) that rise and fall in hills, mountains, cliffs, and valleys. Ravines can cut into the ocean floor and reach down as deep as y=11.

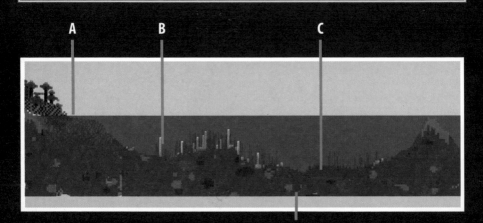

A   B   C

D

Some small patches of the ocean floor rise high, some high enough to form islands. Here, and at the ocean's edges, where the floor rises to meet land, you can find the ground changing from gravel to a mix of stone, patches of clay, sand, and the blocks the land biome is made of, like dirt, sand, and terracotta.

Ocean banks include the ground blocks of the biome they are rising to, like the terracotta blocks of the mesa.

You'll find kelp and seagrass growing on the Ocean biome floor, with some kelp growing up to sea level. You'll also see dolphins, cod, salmon, and squid living in the ocean waters. The drowned, a variant of the zombie hostile mob, can also spawn in the ocean waters. When you are exploring, look out for underwater ruins and shipwrecks, which can appear in any ocean biome, and are great sources for loot and buried treasure maps.

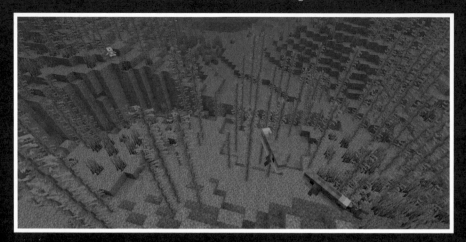

You'll find kelp, cod, shipwrecks, and dolphins in the ocean, not to mention squid and the drowned!

Cold Ocean

The Cold Ocean biome is virtually identical to the Ocean biome, save for it's the darker blue color of its waters. If you are looking for a Frozen Ocean, finding a cold ocean means you are likely close to your goal.

As well as cod, you'll see salmon swimming in small groups in the cold and frozen oceans, as well as rivers.

Frozen Ocean

The water of a Frozen Ocean biome is even darker than the water in a Cold Ocean biome, but much of the water at the surface has frozen to ice. You'll also find icebergs here, some massive, made of blue ice, packed ice, and snow. The temperature can vary in a Frozen ocean: The coldest areas have snowfall instead of rain. In all areas, though, it is too cold for either seagrass or kelp to grow, and dolphins also will not spawn here. You will see salmon, squid and the drowned, of course. Above the ocean on the ice and on icebergs, you will see polar bears and the stray, a variant of the skeleton.

Much of the ocean's surface is covered by ice and icebergs in a frozen ocean.

Lukewarm Ocean

A Lukewarm Ocean has lighter water than a regular ocean and its floor is primarily made of sand blocks. You'll find cod and squid here, along with the pufferfish and tropical fish that need warmer waters.

You know you're entering into a lukewarm ocean when the sea color turns greenish and the ocean floor turns to sand.

Warm Ocean

The Warm Ocean biome is the liveliest and most colorful of the ocean biomes, as it is home to coral reefs, tropical fish, and dolphins, and has a warm green water color. Coral reefs are stretches of the sandy ocean floor that are covered with tree-like outgrowths of red, yellow, pink, magenta, and blue coral blocks and coral fans. Glowing sea pickles grow on coral, illuminating the reef at night.

Warm oceans are even lighter and greener than lukewarm oceans and are home to brightly colored coral reefs.

There are 20 types of live coral in Minecraft. Different shapes are (from top to bottom): Coral, coral fans, coral wall fans, and blocks. Different types, from left to right, are tube (blue), brain (pink), bubble (magenta), fire (red), and horn (yellow). For each of these, there is a "dead" equivalent that is colored in grays. You can use bonemeal on the sandy warm ocean floor to spawn more coral and coral fans (and sea grass).

Sea pickles grow in clumps of 1 (with a light value of 6) to 4 (with a light value of 15) on the floors and on coral blocks of warm oceans. You can use bonemeal on sea pickles to spawn more sea pickles.

Deep Oceans

Except for the Warm Ocean biome, there are Deep variants of all the ocean biomes, except for Warm Oceans. Deep oceans reach to about the y=30 level, deep enough for the rare guardian-infested Ocean Monuments to generate.

Rivers

Rivers in Minecraft have their own unique River biome—the grass color is slightly bluish, and you can see the grass color changing between the river biome and the biome it is next to. Rivers often separate two biomes but they may cut through a single biome. River water reaches the same level as oceans (y=64). They can be as shallow as 1 to 2 blocks or as deep as 9 blocks, with the average river bed at y=56. River beds grow sea grass and are made of dirt, gravel, and sand with occasional patches of clay. Small clusters of sugarcane may grow on the river banks. Squid, salmon, and the drowned spawn in rivers.

River biomes often separate two biomes; here a river separates a savannah biome from a plains biome and a desert biome.

Lakes

Lakes in Minecraft do not have their own biome, but they are unique geographical features and are similar to rivers. They are usually fairly shallow and their beds are also composed of dirt, sand, and gravel, with random patches of clay. They can be found at higher levels than rivers, and occasionally even underground.

Frozen Rivers

The Frozen River biome is a variant of the River biome and have most of the same characteristics. However, you'll only find them in snowy tundra biomes and the frozen river's surface is primarily ice blocks rather than water. Mobs that spawn on frozen rivers are salmon, polar bears, rabbits, the drowned, and strays. Any sugar cane that spawns on a frozen river's banks will usually break and drop if it is next to an ice block rather than water.

You can find salmon beneath the icy surface of a frozen river.

Swamp

Swamp biomes are the flooded lowlands of Minecraft. Part land, but mostly water, swamps feature many tiny patches of land, stretches of low flat land, and expanses of very shallow, gray-green waters. A variant, Swamp Hills, has slightly higher and more varied terrain. Overall, swamps are one of the most unusual of Minecraft biomes, with some features that can't be found anywhere else:

• Swamp oaks: Oaks in swamps have wider canopies than normal (small) oak trees and are covered in vines.

• Swamp witch huts: Swamps are the natural abode of witches. While they can spawn in other biomes, a swamp may have a witch hut, which will spawn a witch with a black cat companion.

• Slimes: Although slimes can spawn below ground in special "slime" chunks, they don't spawn on land anywhere besides swamps.

• Swamp themed villagers: Although villages don't generate in swamps, you can build your own village, and the villagers you bring to live there will sport unique swampland costumes.

• Lily pads

• Blue orchids

Other features you can expect from your visit to a swamp include sugarcane, seagrass, plenty of clay patches in the primarily dirt-block swamp beds, and occasionally a fossil.

As well as greenish water and skies, you may find a rare witch's hut in a swamp, complete with black cat and potted mushroom.

Ocean-adjacent Biomes and Geographical Features

As you explore your world's oceans, you'll also notice some biomes that occur only at the edges of oceans:

• Beach biome: Narrow strips of sand that edge the biomes bordering oceans. Beaches are the natural spawning ground of turtles.

• Snowy Beach biome: Similar to beaches, but with a layer of snow covering the sand.

• Stone Shore biome: Stoney, steep borders that transition between mountains and oceans.

• Mushroom Field Shore biome: Narrow strips of mycelium that may edge the Mushroom Fields biome when it touches ocean and river biomes.

Beach biome

Stone shore biome

Mushroom field shore biome

Snowy beach biome

CHAPTER 2

CREATURES OF THE SEA

Most of the Minecraft creatures that live in and around its oceans are unique to these watery biomes. You'll want to know which mobs to beware of and which to befriend!

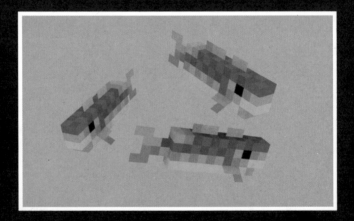

Cod

And you'll be pretty safe around a cod! The cod is a fish found in most oceans (regular, lukewarm, and cold) and rivers of Minecraft. They'll spawn in small groups and swim together in schools of up to 9 cod. They're a good source of early game food as you can kill them pretty easily with a sword. Like any fish, they'll need to be in water to survive.

Type: Passive
Health: 3 HP
Drops: Raw code, bonemeal (rare)

Buckets of Fish

You can pick a cod, salmon, pufferfish, or tropical fish up with a bucket of water to create a "bucket" of that fish. You can make a bucket of cod, a bucket of salmon, a bucket of tropical fish, and a bucket of pufferfish. You can transport and store that fish or use it to drop the fish – just make sure to drop it in water to keep it alive!

A large group of dolphins plays with a red apple, tossing it and then following it again.

Dolphins

Dolphins will spawn in any non-frozen oceans of Minecraft, in groups of 3 to 5, occasionally with a baby dolphin. They'll swim together in small groups as well, jumping in the air and diving back underwater. They need both water and air to survive, and will die if they are submerged without air or left without water. They're a neutral mob, so they will attack you in groups if you attack one of them. Dolphins are one of the most complex creatures in Minecraft and have several interesting behaviors. First, they'll play with you--if you drop an item near them in the water, they'll come to investigate and then start nosing and bouncing the item around. You can feed dolphin raw salmon or cod to earn trust, and the dolphin will lead you to the nearest buried treasure or chest in an underwater ruins or shipwreck. Lastly, if you swim near a dolphin, it will give you five seconds of the "Dolphin's Grace" status effect, which allows you to swim extra fast.

Type: Neutral
Health: 10 HP
Damage: 2 HP (Easy difficulty), 3 HP (Normal difficulty), 4 HP (hard difficulty)
Drops: Raw cod

Drowned

The drowned is the zombie of the seas (and rivers!). They'll spawn in these waters whenever light is lower than 7. They can also spawn as part of an underwater ruins structure, so be careful when you boat or swim by one of these. Like regular zombies, they can spawn as babies and riding chickens as chicken jockies. If you see a chicken floating out in the middle of the ocean – it is likely it was once ridden by a baby drowned!

The Nautilus

In the real world, nautilus are a type of mollusk that live in a distinctive whirling shell and have been around for hundreds of millions of years. Mollusks are a type of invertebrate – animals that don't have spines. Squid are also mollusks. In Mine-craft, you don't see the live nautilus animal, just the shells you can get from fishing or sometimes killing a drowned.

The drowned are the only source of a very powerful weapon, the trident. Not all drowned have tridents (and you may see some with fishing rods!) and even fewer will drop their trident when you kill them. Some drowned may also drop nautilus shells, which are used for crafting conduits. Regular zombies can also become drowned if they are submerged for 45 seconds, but they won't have the same drops as a "born" drowned. Like zombies, the drowned will attack not just you, but also turtle eggs to destroy them and attack villagers, golem, and wandering traders. You're pretty safe with the drowned during the day, however, as they wait until night time to follow and attack you.

Type: Hostile (passive during day)
Health: 20 HP
Damage: 2 HP (Easy), 3 HP (Normal), 4 HP (Hard), with trident 5 (Easy), 9 HP (Normal), 12 (Hard)
Drops: Zombie flesh, nautilus shell, more rarely, gold ingot, trident, nautilus shells

Elder Guardian

The elder guardian is a "mini-boss" of Minecraft and have a much higher health level than skeletons or zombies. They are a variant of the guardian hostile mob, and they are also a limited mob; only three spawn with each ocean monument. You'll usually first run into one with a rare jump scare as you approach an ocean monument. A ghostly image of an elder guardian will suddenly pop on your screen with an eerie moan. It delivers you the warning of a mining fatigue effect to prevent you from easily mining down into the ocean monument and attacking them. The Elder Guardians of an ocean monument regularly check for nearby players, so you'll continue to be given mining fatigue if you cure it by drinking a bucket of milk.

There are three elder guardians at each monument. Two spawn in the two wings of the monument and the third spawns in the top room. In addition to afflicting you with mining fatigue, they attack you with a ranged laser attack and melee spike attack.

You can stop them from firing a laser attack at you by hiding behind blocks.

Type: Hostile
Health: 80 HP
Damage: From laser attacks: 5 HP (Easy), 8 HP (Normal), 12 HP (Hard); from spike attacks, 2 HP.
Drops: Prismarine shards and crystal, wet sponge, raw fish (usually cod)

Bosses
Bosses are especially difficult in-game enemies; they are often single challenges to achieve a special goal in the game. Mini-bosses are less difficult, but still harder to defeat than ordinary hostiles. Other types of bosses in games are super-bosses (even stronger than a boss but often optional side-quests) and a final boss, the boss you must defeat in order to finish or win the game.

Guardian

Guardians are the more common relative of the Elder Guardian and are also found at ocean monuments. They look very similar, and have the same types of attacks (laser and spike) but are a bit smaller and not as strong. You'll also see a lot more of them as they spawn regularly at and around ocean monuments. They attack squid and players, and you'll often hear their buzzing laser attack before you see them.

Type: Hostile
Health: 30 HP
Damage: From laser attacks, 4 HP (Easy), 6 HP (Normal), 9 HP (Hard); from spikes, 2 HP
Drops: Prismarine shards and crystals, raw fish (usually cod)

Polar Bear

The polar bear is an inhabitant of frozen oceans, living atop stretches of surface ice. You can also find them in other snowy and icy biomes. They often spawn with babies, and will attack you if you get too close to their babies or attack them. In fact, nearby polar bears will join in the attack against you! You're not their only enemy; polar bears will also attack any nearby foxes.

Type: Neutral
Health: 30 HP
Damage: 4 HP (Easy), 6 HP (Normal), 9 HP (Hard)
Drops: Raw cod or salmon

...sh swell up when you get too close to them.

fish

...pufferfish is not classed as a hostile mob, but they wil... damage on you if you get too close. They will swell up... r real life pufferfish counterparts and also poison you. Yc... them swimming alone in the warm and lukewarm oc... ...nes.

...e: Passive
...lth: 3 HP
...nage: 2 HP (Easy), 3 HP (Normal), 4 HP (Hard); Poison ef... 7 seconds
...ps: Pufferfish; more rarely bonemeal

Salmon

You can find salmon, a passive Minecraft fish, swimming in groups in cold and frozen oceans and rivers. They come in three sizes-small, regular, and large. In real life, salmon are known to swim upstream to reach their breeding grounds, and in the same manner, Minecraft salmon can also swim up several blocks of water flowing down. Like any Minecraft fish, they can't live out of water.

Type: Passive
Health: 3 HP
Drops: Raw salmon; more rarely, bonemeal

Squid

The 8 tentacled squid have been around since the early days of Minecraft, and for a short while, you could even milk them like a cow! These days, you are only likely to get a squirt of black ink if you attack them. Squid spawn in small groups in rivers and oceans and are the prey of Guardians and Elder Guardians. Their ink sacs are the only source of black dye in Minecraft besides the rare Wither rose.

Type: Passive
Health: 10 HP
Drops: Inksacs

Stray

Strays are the frozen skeletons, dressed in rags, of the cold Minecraft biomes. They only spawn in Frozen Oceans and Rivers and other snowy biomes. Although they behave very much like skeletons, the arrows they shoot are tipped with the Slowness effect. If you are struck, you'll be afflicted by slowness and unable to walk normally or run for 30 seconds

Type: Hostile
Health: 20 HP
Damage: From arrows: 1 -4HP (Easy/Normal), 1-5HP (Hard); from melee: 2 HP (Easy/Normal), 3 HP (Hard)
Drops: Bones, arrows, more rarely, arrows of slowness or other equipment

Tropical Fish

Tropical fish live in the warm and lukewarm oceans, where they spawn in groups and swim in schools of up to 9 fish. With different body shapes, colors, and patterns, this makes for several thousand possible varieties of tropical fish. However, most fish, (up to 90%) that spawn are one of twenty two types of fish, named for real life counterparts. The remaining fish that spawn take on and are named for a random pattern and color.

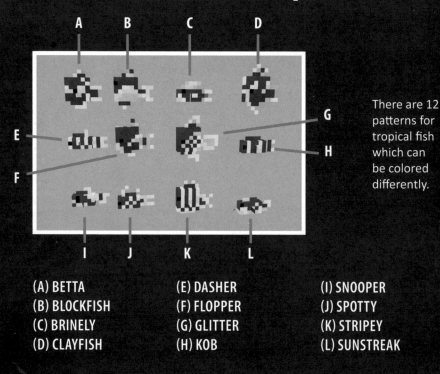

A B C D

E

F

G

H

There are 12 patterns for tropical fish which can be colored differently.

I J K L

(A) BETTA
(B) BLOCKFISH
(C) BRINELY
(D) CLAYFISH

(E) DASHER
(F) FLOPPER
(G) GLITTER
(H) KOB

(I) SNOOPER
(J) SPOTTY
(K) STRIPEY
(L) SUNSTREAK

The twenty two most common types of tropical fish are the anemone (orange-gray stripey), black tang (gray flopper), blue tang (gray-blue flopper), butterfly fish (white-gray clayfish), cichlid (blue-gray sunstreak), clownfish (orange-white kob), cotton candy betta (pink-light blue spotty), dottyback (purple-yellow blockfish), emperor red snapper (white-red clayfish), goatfish (white-yellow spotty), Moorish idol (white-gray glitter), ornate butterflyfish (white-orange clayfish), parrotfish (cyan-pink dasher), queen angelfish (lime-light blue brinely), red cichlid (red-white betty), red lipped blenny (gray-red snooper), red snapper (red-white blockfish), threadfin (white-yellow flopper), tomato clownfish (red-white kob), triggerfish (gray-white sunstreak), yellowtail parrotfish (cyan-yellow dasher), yellow tang (yellow flopper).

Type: Passive
Health: 3 HP
Drops: Tropical fish; more rarely, bonemeal

Turtles

Turtles spawn on Beach biomes, sometimes in small groups and sometimes with a baby turtle. They spend much of their time swimming in the ocean, but they will return to the beach they spawned on to lay their eggs. To breed two turtles, you feed them with seagrass. (Turtles will also follow you if you hold seagrass). Once you've bred two turtles, one will be pregnant and look a bit thicker. The pregnant turtle will return to its home beach, where it digs around on some sand for a bit and then will lay 1 to 4 eggs.

Turtle eggs grow in three stages, each with slightly more cracks in the shell, and you'll hear the cracking sound at each stage. An egg will take several days to hatch. When they do hatch, you'll have a tiny baby turtle – the smallest mobs in Minecraft! You can feed

baby turtles seagrass to grow up more quickly, and when they do, they'll drop a scute — a scale from their growing shell. You can use five scutes to craft a turtle shell you can wear as a helmet which will give you ten more seconds of underwater breathing. A turtle shell gives you the same amount of protection as an iron helmet and can also be enchanted and has better durability.

Type: Passive
Health: 30 HP
Drops: Seagrass

CHAPTER 3

OCEAN MONUMENTS

cean Monuments, along with coral reefs, are one of the top destination spots of Minecraft's oceans. Conquering one is good for bragging rights, plus it's the only place to get a lot of some of the rarest blocks--prismarine, dark prismarine, prismarine bricks, and sea lanterns--that ocean monuments are made from.

There's a stash of shiny gold blocks to loot, and if you fully explore the monument, you may also find a hidden room holding the rare sponge block. Finally, a conquered ocean monument is an opportunity to build an enormous guardian farm for amassing their drops of the rare prismarine crystals.

Ocean monuments are the home of three elder guardians and a host of regular guardians. The three elder guardians only spawn once with each monument, but guardians will keep respawning in the ocean monument area. You'll also see squid here, with the guardians eagerly attacking them.

Ocean monuments are only spawned in deep variants of ocean biomes, because they are so tall. The main structure is 22 blocks high, reaching up to just two blocks below sea level. The 58 by 58 building is held up by 23 4 by 4 massive pillars that reach to the ocean floor.

Finding an Ocean Monument

You can spot ocean monuments fairly easily, and especially at night, by the shape of the top arches near to sea level, and the light coming from these and the entranceway arches. Monuments can be rare, so if you are having difficulty finding one, you can trade a Cartographer villager for an ocean explorer map for some emeralds and a compass.

You can spot monuments at night from the light glowing near the surface.

If you are playing in creative mode, you can find an ocean monument using the **/locate monument** command. This will find the nearest monument to you. If you want to find more monuments, you'll need to move further away to try the command again.

In creative mode, type in /locate, add a space, and a list of possible locations shows. You can click the one you want, and a location will show in chat. You'll then have to click that location shown in chat, and a teleport command will appear. You'll then need to press Enter to execute the teleport command.

Another way to find ocean monuments is through online seed analyzers, like Chunkbase.com. These use the Minecraft algorithms and your world seed to locate generated structures and features, like spawn chunks, villages, jungle pyramids, and ocean monuments. To find out your world seed, use the command **/seed**.

USING AN OCEAN EXPLORER MAP

A brand new explorer map will show the outlines of a region and always points north. An icon shows where the monument is, and a white icon shows where you are in relation to this. If you are very far away (further than about 1000 blocks) your icon will be very small. As you near the map's region, your icon changes to a bigger size. Finally, when you enter the 512 by 512 block region shown by the map, your icon will change into a pointer and the map will start coloring in around you.

Inside the monument are a variety of randomly generated rooms, but you can always count on a few regular features, beyond the arched entranceway and supporting columns.

1. Top room. The very top room of the monument houses one elder guardian.

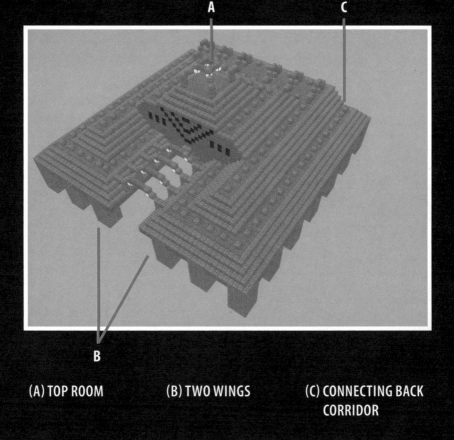

A

C

B

(A) TOP ROOM **(B) TWO WINGS** **(C) CONNECTING BACK CORRIDOR**

2. Two wings. The two wings of the monument each house an elder guardian. One of the wings has a plus-shaped column of prismarine at the front end, and the other will have an 8x9 platform raised on four 1x1 pillars, and with a central 3x3 column atop it.

3. Back corridor. The two wings of the monument are connected by a narrow corridor that runs along the back.

4. Treasure room. In the center of the monument is a two-storey high room that contains a tall structure made with dark prismarine. Behind the dark prismarine blocks are 8 blocks of gold. Presumably, this is what the guardians guard!

In between and among these rooms and three floors, you'll find a confusing maze of corridors and rooms. If you are lucky, there will somewhere be a sponge room – a room with several and sometimes many sponge blocks. You can sometimes even find two, even three, sponge rooms in a monument.

SPONGES

Sponges are a great way to remove multiple blocks of water at a time, if you are clearing up underwater areas to make them livable (Like an ocean monument!) You just click a dry sponge (you dry used, wet sponges in a furnace) against a surface underwater, and nearby water blocks, in a radius of about 7 blocks) will be "absorbed".

Conquering a Monument

There are many ways to conquer a monument and different ideas about what this means. You may just want to loot the sponges, some prismarine, and the gold, or you may want to clear it of all hostile guardians and make it your new base.

One of the main obstacles of raising a monument is the Mining Fatigue effect that the three elder guardians will cast on you. This slows down your mining speed, making it nearly impossible to break blocks. Every minute, the Elder Guardian will search for any player within 50 blocks, even invisible players, and cast this effect on them. You can drink milk to negate the effect once it is cast, but you will still only have under a minute to break blocks. This means an efficient raid on a monument will involve killing the Elder Guardians as quickly as possible.

The elder guardian apparition shows up on your screen suddenly to deliver you Mining Fatigue.

1. Enchant Your Armor!
You'll be underwater, so enchant your helmet with the strongest level of Respiration that you can to extend the time you can breathe underwater. You also want your helmet to have the Aqua Affinity enchantment, to improve underwater mining speed. Ordinarily (without the Elder Guardian's Mining Fatigue effect), your mining speed underwater is about five times slower – its possible to mine, it just takes a long time. Aqua Affinity lets you mine at a normal speed underwater. And on all of your armor, you'll want the highest level of Protection you can afford. Finally, enchant your boots with Depth Strider, so you can move much more quickly below water.

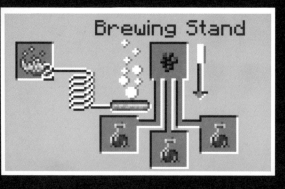

You make awkward potion in a brewing stand powered with blaze powder.

New to Brewing?

To make potions, you'll need a brewing stand, blaze powder, nether wart, glass bottles, and ingredients for the specific potion. Make the starter "awkward" potion by brewing nether wart into glass bottles of water. Then brew the awkward potions with potion ingredients to create the base potions. For Water Breathing, use a pufferfish and for Night Vision, use a golden carrot. For Invisibility potion, you'll need to brew a fermented spider eye (a spider eye crafted with sugar and a brown mushroom) into a Night Vision potion. Once you have your potions, you can brew them again with redstone dust to extend the time the potion lasts from 3 minutes to 8 minutes.

To brew a final potion, brew your awkward potions with an ingredient like a pufferfish.

2. Prepare Your Potions

Invisibility potions can be incredibly handy – although you have to remove your armor for them to be fully effective. A mob can still detect you if you get very close. According to the official Minecraft wiki, at minecraft.gamepedia.com, invisibility reduces detection distance to about 7 percent of the original distance, and if you wear armor, to about 17.5 percent. Most mobs can detect you within 16 blocks, so this means without armor, you'll want to stay a couple blocks away to avoid detection, and with armor, about three blocks away. The potion of Water Breathing is also a huge help, giving you from three to eight minutes of breathing underwater. Also consider using potions of Night Vision, to make the ocean depths even brighter.

3. Sharpen Your Weapons

If you can swing it, the best weapon for fighting guardians is a trident enchanted with Impaling and Loyalty.

Best is Trident with Impaling (extra damage) and Loyalty (the trident returns automatically to you). This is a hard –to-get weapon, though, and the next best choice is the strongest sword you can get – if possible a diamond sword with Sharpness IV or V and sweeping edge. Taking a bow as your only weapons isn't a great choice, as arrows are slow underwater and inflict less damage. However, the spikes on guardians give a hefty Thorns attack, and using a bow and arrow does mean you can keep your distance from them. If you have the room, then a bow can make for a useful secondary weapon.

4. Gather More Tools

Other tools that can be incredibly helpful are:

Buckets of milk. These will remove the Elder Guardian's Mining Fatigue potion (but also any other potion effects)

Place a door down to create an airspace

Doors. Placing doors down inside the temple can give you safe breathing spaces as well as block guardians from seeing and attacking you. A half stack of doors can be a life saver.

Conduit and kelp. Because the monument is built from prismarine, it is very easy to place a conduit and create conduit power. Kelp (the plant, not dried kelp blocks) is a great block to place down first on a surface, allowing you to place the conduit easily on top of the kelp. Kelp is a block that you can easily remove even with Mining Fatigue.

Boat(s). For ocean transport, of course!

Food. For regeneration health during battle.

Bed, Backup supplies, Ender chest. In any battle that might kill you, you will want to create a protected spawn point near the battle. This way you can re-arm and get back to the battle to retrieve your stuff (and continue the fight!)

5. Establish Your Safe Base

Before you raid the monument, establish your safe base near the monument, where you can keep a bed and your backup supplies. "Safe" means somewhere you can get to quickly or respawn at where you won't be attacked by guardians. So you'll want a nearby island or a platform with some barriers to hide you from view and laser attacks. To set up a platform in the middle of the ocean, you can place blocks on top of sea-level kelp or bring along a lily pad you can build on. Remember that if your base is within 50 blocks of the monument, you can be afflicted with Mining Fatigue.

Attack Plans

If your raid involves killing the Elder Guardians, you'll want to tackle them first. You can often break into the top room of the monument, where one Elder Guardian lives, before being given Mining Fatigue. Another tactic, if you've been hampered by Mining Fatigue, is to place a block of TNT on the monument's top, then

surround the TNT's four sides with other blocks. Finally, set off the TNT by placing a redstone block on its top. Because all of the TNT's sides are covered by blocks, it can explode, and this will give you entry into the monument.

Inside the monument, kill the Elder Guardian in the top room, then go to the wings of the monument to kill the other two. If you are swimming on the outside, you can often see Elder Guardians partly glitching through the monument walls.

Using a Conduit

Because there's so much prismarine in the monument, you can activate a conduit pretty easily to bring you the conduit's effects of underwater breathing, night vision, and improved mining speed. You'll want to place a conduit in the middle of a cube of water that's at least 3x3x3 blocks. Use a kelp plant to place the conduit on (kelp is a block that is easy to break under Mining Fatigue). For example, look for a location that is a block away from a floor, a ceiling, and a wall. Placing a conduit here will enable many blocks

Place a conduit a block away from a wall, floor, and ceiling to activate conduit power.

in the floor, ceiling, and wall to act as conduit enabling blocks—
you'll need 16 blocks within the 5x5 conduit frame to power up
the conduit. See Chapter 5 for more on conduits.

Locating the Treasure Room

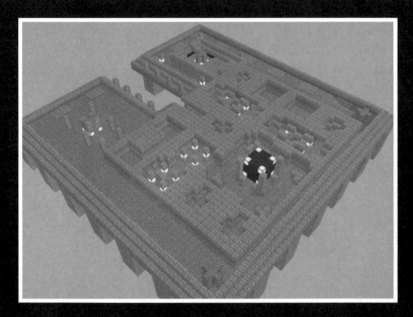

The treasure room can be found at the back of the monument but it may be to the
left, middle, or right.

The Treasure Room One way to find the treasure room easily is to first locate the corridor at the back of the monument
that joins the two wings. The treasure room will be somewhere
along this corridor. It's quite big, so you can usually find it after
knocking a few places in the corridor's interior wall.

Finding the Sponge Room

Searching for the sponge room(s) can be a bit trickier. They are low-ceilinged rooms that are entered from a 2x2 hole in their floor, so look up as you swim about. You'll often find a sponge room on the top floor along the same wing that houses the large Elder Guardian platform. The second place to look is near the front of the monument, away from the large treasure room. If you are playing with cheats on, turn on Spectator mode (/gamemode spectator) to pass directly through walls.

This ocean monument housed three sponge rooms, two along one wing, and one to the front.

CHAPTER 4
LOOTING THE HIGH SEAS

One of the best features (I think!) of Minecraft's oceans is the loot you can get just from boating around, checking out shipwrecks, exploring underwater ruins, feeding dolphins, following treasure maps, and digging for buried chests in the sand.

There are three main looting locales in the oceans: Shipwrecks, underwater ruins, and buried treasure. Shipwrecks and underwater ruins are fairly easy to spot when you boat around your oceans. To find buried treasure, you must first have a buried treasure map, which you can find in both shipwreck map chests and in the chests at underwater ruins.

You can also choose to partner up with some local dolphins. If you feed a dolphin raw cod or salmon, it will guide you to the nearest loot chest – this may be in a shipwreck, hidden in an ocean ruin, or buried along the shore. Once you've located a dolphin-found chest, you can break it, and the dolphin will then be able to find the next nearest loot chest.

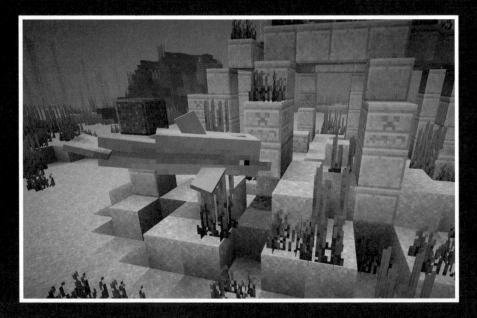

In return for a snack, a dolphin will lead you to the nearest treasure.

Shipwrecks

Shipwrecks are full or partial ship structures you can find underneath the waves or just partially submerged. The game randomly generates these throughout the world in ocean biomes and more rarely in beach biomes. They all conform to the same standard shape, but many generate with sections removed; tilted on their side or upside down. Different ships are also built with different combinations of planks and logs.

A fully generated shipwreck has three chests to loot. These are the supply chest, the map chest, and the treasure chest, and they're always located in the same spots below deck (unless the ship has only generated partially, in which case one or more chests may also be missing). Here's where you can find them and what you're likely to find in them:

A B C　　　D　　　　　E　　　　　　F

(A) STERN　　　　　(C) RUDDER　　　　(E) SUPPLY CHEST
(B) TREASURE CHEST　(D) MAP CHEST　　　(F) BOW

• **Supply chest.** You'll find the supply chest in the bow of the ship (the front), and it contains items related to food, clothing, ship maintenance, and battling. Loot here may be carrots, wheat, potatoes, rotten flesh, pumpkins, bamboo, suspicious stew, paper, gunpowder, coal, TNT, and enchanted leather armor.

• **Map chest.** The map chest is located in the stern (back) of the ship on the lowest level – the same level as the supply chest. It stores random items related to mapmaking, book making, and navigating: paper, feathers, books, clock, compass, empty maps. You'll always find a buried treasure map in the map chest, which will lead you to a chest of loot buried on a beach somewhere.

• **Treasure chest.** The treasure chest is also in the stern (back) of the ship, on the top level, and above the rudder. It contains the presumable booty from the ships long-gone pirates: iron, gold, diamonds, lapis, emeralds, and bottles o' enchanting. Aaar!

SUSPICIOUS STEW

This stew certainly sounds suspicious, and it has purplish and green blobs in it. There's no telling what it will do when you eat it. Depending on what the galley cook threw in, you may get one of 9 status effects that last a few seconds, but not all of them are good. You can brew up some of this stew yourself and you'll know what it will do. Suspicious stew is the same recipe as mushroom stew (a wooden bowl, a red mushroom and a brown mushroom), except you add in a flower. The type of flower you add is what gives the stew its status effect.

- Allium: Fire resistance
- Azure Bluet: Blindness
- Blue Orchid or Dandelion: Saturation
- Cornflower: Jump boost
- Lily of the Valley: Poison
- Oxeye Daisy: Regeneration
- Poppy: Night Vision
- Tulip: Weakness
- Wither Rose: Wither

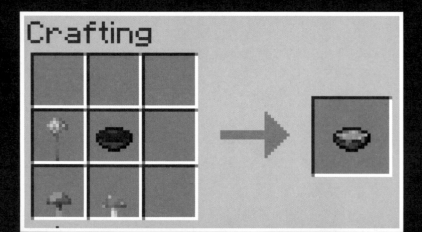

Although shipwrecks often look temptingly like they'll be easy to loot, it's very easy to get stuck and a bit turned around in them, just enough to start drowning. Potions of Water Breathing and Night Vision can help, as can boots with Depth Strider and a helmet with Respiration. In addition, a helmet with the Aqua Affinity enchantment and an axe with Efficiency will help you hack through ship walls and trapdoors both to get at the chest and to get out.

Underwater Ruins

Spend a little time swimming with the dolphins below the waves, and you'll see mysterious structures populating the ocean floor. Look a little closer, and you'll see these are abandoned buildings and small villages – often accompanied by a hostile drowned zombie or two. You can find these ruins in any ocean biome (and rarely on the shore) and most importantly – almost all of these buildings include a loot chest! In addition, you can find some rare blocks like prismarine also in these structures.

There are two types of underwater ruins: cold ocean and warm ocean. Cold ocean underwater ruins are generated in oceans with gravel sea beds: regular, cold, and frozen oceans. These ruins are built mostly from stone brick. The warm ocean ruins are found on the sandy floors of lukewarm and warm oceans and they are built primarily out of sandstone. All in all, there are 16 different structures for cold ocean ruins and 32 for warm ocean ruins. In addition to the loot chests, underwater ruins can be a source for different and rare building materials:

• **Cold Ocean Underwater Ruins.** These structures may contain mossy cobblestone, mossy stone bricks, stone brick stairs, cracked stone bricks, chiseled stone bricks, regular bricks, spruce and dark oak planks, polished granite, purple glazed terracotta, spruce and dark oak planks, magma blocks, obsidian, prismarine, and sea lanterns.

• **Warm Ocean Underwater Ruins.** At these ruins, you may find cut sandstone, chiseled sandstone, sandstone stairs, polished diorite, polished granite, light blue terracotta, magma blocks, and sea lanterns.

There are 24 different structures for small, cold ocean underwater ruins and 8 for small, warm ocean ruins. Some of the differences are slight, and the structures may also generate with further "ruination", missing additional blocks.

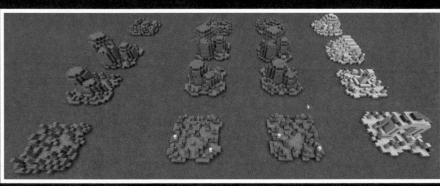

There are 12 different structures for big ruins in cold oceans and 4 big ruins struc-

When you're boating, you'll usually notice an underwater ruin by the light and bubbles coming from the occasional magma block that the structure includes. As the ruins are on the ocean floor and often very deep, you'll want all the help you can get from potions and enchanted armor to loot them. Also remember to bring buried weapons, as drowned often generate with a ruins structure, along with (not necessarily alongside). However, the generation of the ruins structures often removes random blocks as part of their "ruination" and this process may also remove a loot chest and/or a drowned spawn point.

Abandoned ruins loot contain a random assortment of goods that includes coal, wheat, rotten flesh, emeralds, golden apples, buried treasure maps, enchanted fishing rods, enchanted books, leather tunics, stone axes, and gold helmets.

Underwater Ruins

Spend a little time swimming with the dolphins below the waves, and you'll see mysterious structures populating the ocean floor. Look a little closer, and you'll see these are abandoned buildings and small villages – often accompanied by a hostile drowned zombie or two. You can find these ruins in any ocean biome (and rarely on the shore) and most importantly – almost all of these buildings include a loot chest! In addition, you can find some rare blocks like prismarine also in these structures.

Place your pointer at the bottom of the X to locate buried treasure.

To find buried treasure, you'll need a buried treasure map from a shipwreck or under-water ruins, or the help of a dolphin! Even then, it can be pretty tricky to find the actual chest. The map will give you a general "X" marks the spot as to the location, and the location will always be either on a beach or underwater beside a beach, or on the side of a shallow underwater hill. It is usually buried under sand, but occasionally under gravel and more rarely stone. The X on the map is pretty big however, and covers a lot of blocks. Position yourself on the map so that the point of your pointer shows just below the center of the X, and dig down.

Buried treasure chests always contain a heart of the sea, along with a random assortment of loot which may be iron, gold, diamonds, emeralds, prismarine crystals, cooked cod or salmon, TNT, and iron swords.

As you explore the oceans looking for loot, keep an eye out for any bright, lit area coming from beneath the waves. The light can be coming from ruins or other struc tures, like this abandoned mineshaft extending just above the ocean floor.

CHAPTER 5
AQUATIC SURVIVAL SKILLS

dventuring is how you will get the best loot in the game (ores and diamonds), but for a price: the risk of losing your inventory by "dying" to mob battle. Each adventure is a special buildplate that you place and explore. But adventures don't have a "Pickup" mode - you'll be interacting with these worlds in much the same way you interact with world in the original Minecraft game. This means you'll need the right tool to break blocks, and using the wrong tool can mean it either takes a very long time to break or that it will just disappear after being broken: no resource given. You'll need a stone or iron pick to mine ore, a wood pick or better to mine stone and cobblestone, and a sword to fight mobs like spiders, skeletons, and creepers.

Ocean Nutrition

The best very-early game food is kelp; it grows quickly and abundantly in most oceans and requires almost no effort to collect a lot. Break kelp plants at the second block up from the ocean bed so that the plant continues to grow. You can collect the floating, broken kelp on the surface and toast them in your furnace or smoker for some dried kelp munchies. Each dried kelp piece only gives you back 1 hunger point (0.5 haunch on your HUD (heads up display), but you can eat this food faster than any other.

Kelp is abundant in the oceans and is a great starting game food.

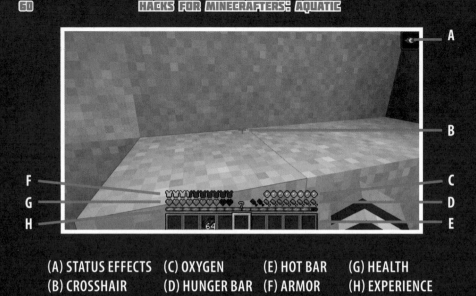

(A) STATUS EFFECTS   (C) OXYGEN   (E) HOT BAR   (G) HEALTH
(B) CROSSHAIR   (D) HUNGER BAR   (F) ARMOR   (H) EXPERIENCE

Once you are a little more established with a sword, you'll want to kill cod or salmon for much better nutrition. Both fish have 3 HP (1.5 hearts) and just a wooden sword deals 4 HP in damage, so each swing should net you a fish.

If you are hankering for some variety, some veggies, or a vegetarian lifestyle, explore the oceans for shipwrecks. In their supplies chests, you can often find wheat, potatoes, carrots, and if you're willing to risk it, suspicious stew.

Saturation

There is a hidden hunger variable called saturation that affects how fast your hunger bar decreases. Each food is given a certain amount of saturation, and eating foods with higher saturation values will keep your hunger bar fuller for longer.

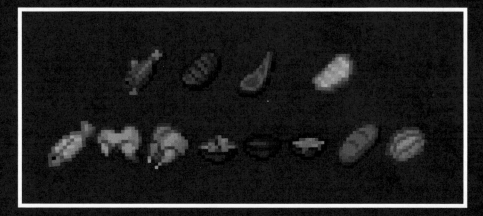

The most filling (of hunger bars) and saturating foods (outside of golden apples and carrots) are on the top row: Cooked mutton, cooked porkchop, steak, and cooked salmon. On the bottom row, are the next best for filling you up: Baked potatoes, beet soup, bread, carrots, cooked chicken, cooked cod, cooked rabbit, mushroom stew, rabbit stew, and suspicious stew.

Ores and Mining

Just as on land, you'll want to be gearing up with good armor and weapons, and for the most part, and that means gathering iron and coal.

The ocean floor and edges are spotted with patches of stone, so you'll find ores underwater occasionally, coal, iron, and sometimes even gold near a Mesa biome. You'll have better luck of course investigating the underwater ravines and caves, once you've solved the breathing under water problem!

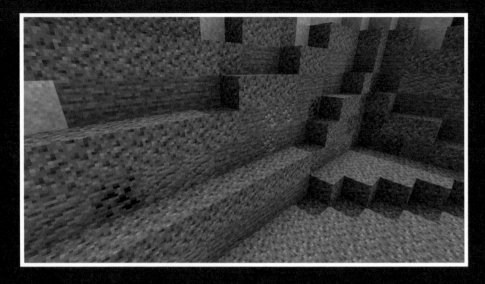

You'll can find some ores in the exposed stone on ocean beds and banks.

Because mining just a single block underwater takes much longer than regular mining, you'll want a helmet enchanted with Aqua Affinity, which removes this impediment. A pickaxed enchanted with Efficiency will also help.

Other ways to get ores include raiding shipwrecks and finding buried treasure. And of course, if you are challenging yourself with desert island survival, you'll be able to dig right down on your island.

Breathing Underwater

As soon as you venture underwater, your HUD (heads up display) will show a row of oxygen bubbles that indicate how much oxygen you have left until you start drowning and taking damage. It takes about 15 seconds until you are depleted of oxygen. There are a number of ways you can extend this time or replenish your oxygen underwater:

- **Doors.** Placing a door underwater creates a pocket of air you can breathe in. It's also good for breaking a guardian's line of sight to you. Fence gates also work, but you have to place them at your head level.

- **Magma blocks.** A magma block produces a stream of oxygen above it. You can place on down and hold shift to step on it to replenish your oxygen. (Soul sand blocks also make these bubbles, but they'll also shoot you up to the surface!)

- **Turtle shells.** When Minecraft baby turtles grow up to adults, they drop a green scale called scute. Breed turtles and collect 5 scutes to craft a turtle shell, which you can use as a helmet. The turtle shell will add 10 seconds of water breathing to make a total of 25 seconds you can stay underwater.

- **Respiration enchantment.** Enchant your helmet or turtle shell with Respiration I, II, or III. Each level gives you 15 additional seconds of underwater breathing, along with a chance to not take damage every second once your oxygen bar has run out.

- **Potion of Water Breathing.** Brew awkward potion with a pufferfish for the Potion of Water Breathing, which grants 3 minutes of underwater breathing. Re-brew the 3-minute potion with redstone dust for an extended Potion of Water Breathing that lasts a full 8 minutes.

- **Conduit.** Building a powered conduit will not only give you underwater breathing, but also faster mining and better vision while you are in its radius. See the Conduit section in chapter 6 for all about these structures and how to build them.

- **Bucket.** Using a bucket repeatedly (right clicking against a surface) underwater. This action removes, for a split second, a water source and replaces it with air. You have to click very quickly up to 40 times to fully replenish your oxygen bar from 0.

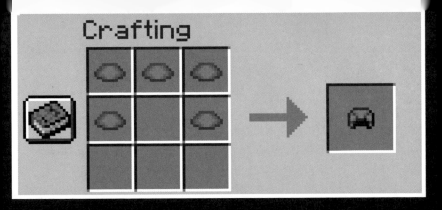

An early game aid for underwater breathing is a turtle shell.

Walking on Water

If you want to make your way across the ocean without boating, enchanting your boots with Frost Walker will turn water temporarily into frosted ice blocks as long as you are walking. Higher levels of this enchantment increases the radius of ice around you.

Fishing

Fishing is a great, but slow, way to get resources from the sea. Besides getting fish for food, it is a decent way to get enchanted books pretty much for free. You'll also get some experience points for each successful catch. What will you catch? One of the following:

• **Fish:** Raw cod, salmon, pufferfish, or tropical fish.

• **Junk:** bamboo, bones, bowls, cocoa beans, damaged fishing rods, ink sacs, leather, leather boots, lily pads, rotten flesh, sticks, string, tripwire hooks, and water bottles.

• **Treasure:** Enchanted bows and fishing rods, enchanted books, nautilus shells, saddles, and name tags.

It does take a bit of time – once you've cast your rod, it will be anywhere from five to 30 seconds until a wavy line of bubbles forms and weaves its way towards your bobber. (If you're new to fishing, then the time to reel in your bounty is when your bobber dips underwater.) If it's raining, you'll wait less time, and if you are fishing without sky access, you'll wait longer.

You can improve all this by using an enchanted fishing rod. Enchantments for your rod include:

- **Luck of the Sea I, II, and III:** Each level of this enchantment increase the chances of getting treasure. (Fishing rods only.)

- **Lure I, II, and III:** Each level of this enchantment decrease the time it takes to get a catch. (Fishing rods only.)

- **Unbreaking I, II, and III:** Each level increases the odds that using the fishing rod won't take durability. (Tools, weapons, and armor.)

- **Mending:** This mends an item you're holding is slowly repaired by experience points (XP).

The Almighty Trident

The trident is one of the most powerful weapons in the game, if it is fully enchanted. You can only get them from killing the Drowned, and even then, Drowned drop them pretty rarely. According to the official Minecraft Wikipedia (Minecraft.gamepedia.com), about 6 % of Drowned spawn with a trident, and even then, there's only aabout a 5 percent chance they'll drop it when you kill them. You'll improve this chance by using a sword with the Looting I, II, or III enchantment.

You can use a trident either as a melee weapon (hitting the mob in front of you) or as a ranged weapon (charging it up like a bow and then releasing it to fly at a distant opponent. Water doesn't slow the trident down in the way it does arrows, but unless you have the Loyalty enchantment, you will need to retrieve a thrown trident. As a melee weapon, an unenchanted trident gives 9 HP of damage, and as a ranged weapon, 8 HP.

Tridents can be enchanted with unbreaking and mending, as with most weapons and tools, and there are also several special trident-only enchantments:

• **Channeling:** This will summon a lightning strike on the target mob as long as there is a thunderstorm ongoing. (Can't be used with Riptide.)

• **Impaling:** Gives extra damage to aquatic mobs excluding the Drowned, who are categorized by the game as Undead.

• **Loyalty:** Your trident will return to you after it hits the target. (Can't be used with Riptide.)

• **Riptide:** This will propel you through the air, as long as you start out in water or if it is raining. (Can't use with Channelling or Loyalty.)

A trident with the channeling enchantment will bring a lightning bolt down upon your target, and turn a villager into a witch.

The riptide enchantment will send you with your trident hurtling through the air.

Minecraft's achievement system covers all aspects of the game, and fulfilling all achievements can be a great way to learn the game, if you are new to Minecraft, or just get some bragging rights. However, if you're interested in your aquatic prowess, there are only a couple of advancements to achieve: (1) Fishy Business: Catch a fish with a fishing rod and (2) Tactical Fishing: Catch a fish with a bucket of water.

If you enjoy challenges, here are some more unofficial aquatic goals you can achieve on your way to conquering the oceans wild.

- Visit every ocean biome.

- Build an aquarium and fill it with five different tropical fish.

- Collect the 22 types of common tropical fish.

- Collect 5 uncommon or rare tropical fish.

- Play bounce the item around with a dolphin.

- Catch a pufferfish with a bucket of water.

- Build an underwater house.

- Loot an ocean monument of its gold and sponges.

- Loot 10 shipwrecks, 10 underwater ruins, and 10 buried treasure.

- Have a dolphin lead you to a treasure chest.

- Swim with a dolphin to get the Dolphin's Grace effect.

- Get a trident and enchant it with loyalty.

- Battle a drowned with your trident.

- Meet and survive an encounter with strays.

- Use a trident with the riptide enchantment.

- Use a trident with the channeling enchantment to attack a mob with lightning. Extra points if you turn a villager into a witch with this!

- Build and power a conduit.

For the ultimate ocean survival bragging rights, try deserted island survival (you can only live on the island or at sea) or a waterworld survival (surviving in the oceans without ever going to land). You can find seeds online for survival islands, and watch videos of other Minecrafters attempt the same challenges on Youtube. Good luck!

CHAPTER 6

BUILDING AT SEA

onstructing anything major at sea or underwater is a challenge, but there are ways to make it easier, and concepts that may give you inspiration for unique buildings. First of all, you need to make the process of building a lot easier, and you can do that with a conduit.

Conduits

The conduit in the center is activated by the square of 16 prismarine around it; the conduit to the left doesn't have enough prismarine in its activation frame area to activate it.

The three biggest problems in underwater building are:

- Breathing underwater (i.e. you can't without help!)

- Mining underwater (this is very slow, normally)

- Seeing underwater (it's dark under there!)

These problems are all solvable with a conduit. Conduits are a must have for any longish term underwater endeavor, whether it's constructing a guardian farm or building your own underwater base. The word "conduit" refers to both the central block used in the structure as well as the entire structure. The conduit block is created from crafting a Heart of the Sea (found in buried treasure chests) with 8 nautilus shells (drops from the Drowned or loot from fishing). By itself, it does nothing, but surround it with an activation frame, and it will power up and deliver Conduit Power to you, as long as you are within range.

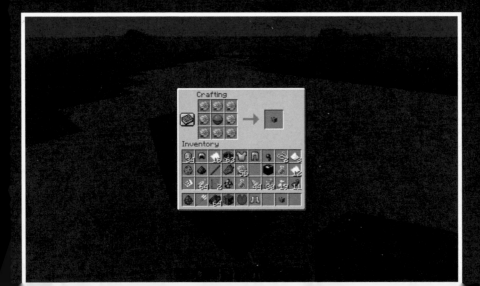

Conduit power bestows the ability to breathe underwater, faster underwater mining speed, and brightens the underwater for greater visibility. You can actually place a conduit anywhere in the world, as long as the center 3x3 cube is filled with water, but its effects are only really useful underwater.

Conduit power will also damage any nearby hostile mobs, but only within an 8 block range, and as long as the mobs are in water or in rain. It also only attacks 1 mob at a time.

The range that conduit power reaches depends on the number of blocks used in its frame. A full frame is made of three 5x5 square frames placed around the conduit block. Two squares are vertical and at right angles to each other and the third is horizontal. You'll need at least 1 square frame, or 16 blocks placed in any of the frame area blocks, to power up the conduit. This will create an initial range of 32 blocks. From here, you can add sets of 7 blocks to increase the range an additional 16 blocks with each set. The biggest range you can create is 96 blocks of conduit power by using the full 42 blocks in the frame area. This is a massive area you can easily build a mega-underwater base in.

Conduits with one, two, and three activation frame squares. The three-framed conduit uses all block locations for activating the conduit.

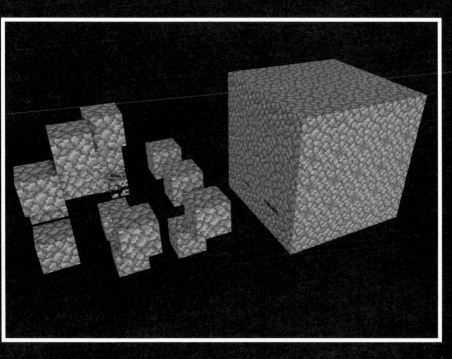

A conduit can be activated by 16 prismarine variants (or sea lanterns) in any of the activation frame locations. Blocks can also be placed in any location of the overall 5x5x5 cubic frame, but if they are not in any of the 3 square frame areas, they won't contribute to activation.

Building a Base

If you are committed to an underwater or sea-faring lifestyle, you have a number of early game options for starter homes. You can use a shipwreck as your first shelter. If it's underwater, you'll want to section off areas and use an easy-to-break block like sand or gravel to remove interior water blocks.

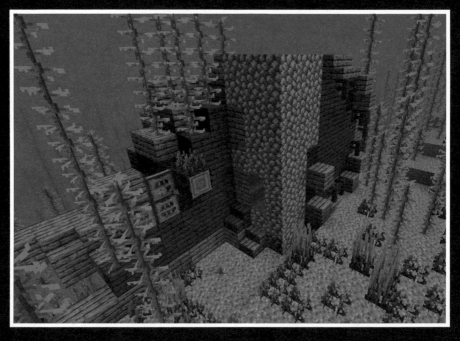

If you're intent on a strict ocean survival, a shipwreck close to the surface makes a great starting base.

Boat Power

If you're in danger of starving at sea, climb into a boat. While you're in a boat, you won't lose any hunger points, so you can use the boat to fish from or make an emergency trip to shore.

Or you can raid a shipwreck for its wood (and loot of course), craft some doors, and use these for oxygen to help you mine into an underwater hill for your first cubby hole or underwater hobbit hole. If you stand in the doorspace of a door placed underwater, you can actually mine at regular speed.

If your goal is a standalone underwater abode, there are several ways to go about it. Before conduits, a primary way of creating underwater buildings was to create a filled-in sand replica of the shape you wanted on a platform above the water and then break the platform. The sand then falls down to the ocean floor, and you can place blocks around it to create walls and ceilings, and then dig out the central sand blocks to create the breathable interior space.

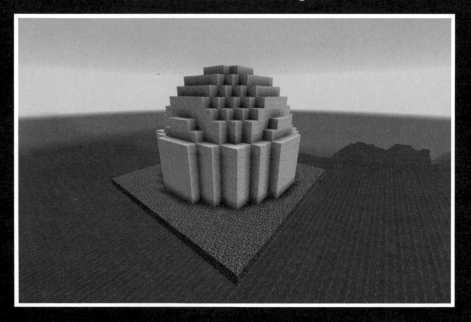

For the platform method to work, the ocean floor beneath must be flat.

With a conduit in place, you can swim about, placing and mining blocks as you need for the walls and ceilings and floor. You will still need a way to remove the water from the interior of the building. The fastest way to do this is with sponge blocks that you can loot from an ocean monument. If you don't have these, you'll want to fill the interior with sand or gravel or dirt, and then break these.

If you're unsure what kind of underwater base "works", you can build anything you could on land – from castles to hobbit holes; but just understand the difficulties in creating breathable spaces. That said, some buildings might seem more "watery" than others, like underwater holiday resorts, scientific research stations, evil overlord lairs, environmental biospheres, submarine waystations, aquatic zoos and aquariums.

When you're planning an underwater base, some things to consider are:

- **Crops and farming.** Will you want areas to farm crops or animals? Do you want to be totally self sufficient living under water?

- **Entryways.** How easy is it to enter and leave? Should entry ways be like doors or do you want to swim up to a floor? Do you want easy access to boats? Can you use bubble columns to enter or leave your home?

- **Visibility.** Do you want to see though glass walls at the ocean around you? If so you may want to locate near a brightly colored coral reef? Or maybe you want a hidden underwater base, which you can disguise with kelp and sea grass?

Animal Transport

If you are planning a self-sufficient underwater base, with animal farming and everything, you'll need a way to get your cows, sheep, pigs, and chickens to your base. First off, it's pretty easy to get them into a boat on land and then hop into the boat yourself and get the three of you to water. (Your path to the water must all be downhill, as boats won't jump up blocks!)

At your base, you will need some kind of a walled in tower reaching from your base beneath water to the surface. It should be constructed so you can push the animal (or the entire boat) into it and the animal will drop. At the bottom of the tower, place a landing area of a one-block deep pool of water. This will prevent the animal from any fall damage.

To transport animals, you can boat them to a constructed drop that connects to your base.

Infinite Water Removal

Minecraft water has a special ability: If you place two blocks of water one block apart from each other or diagonal to each other, these two blocks will create more water source blocks (as opposed to flowing water) between them. However, this makes it tricky when you are removing large areas of water. Depending on your tactic, some or many of the water blocks left will combine to create more water, filling up some of the space you removed. If you're having trouble, start at the top of the water you want to remove or section it off into smaller areas to prevent the infinite water effect.

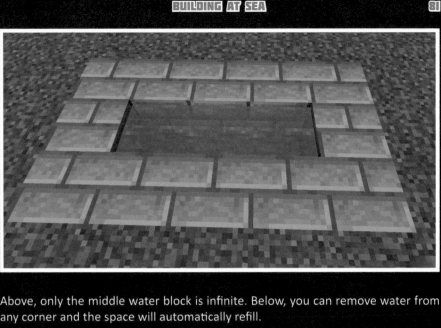

Above, only the middle water block is infinite. Below, you can remove water from any corner and the space will automatically refill.

Bubble-vators

Water makes an excellent down or up elevator in Minecraft. Bubble elevators, or bubble-vators, use soul sand or magma blocks to push you. In water, soul sand will create a column of bubbles that pushes you to the surface of water. Similarly, a magma block will pull down entities caught in its bubble column. The magma block will damage you unless you sneak (shift) while you are on it.

To make an "up" bubble-vator for your own personal use, create a glassed in column of water blocks 1 block square. At the bottom, place a block of soul sand, and at the top of the column of water place a platform to step out onto. Do the same for a "down" bubble-vator, except use a magma block at the bottom. You can use signs in the bottom doorways to stop water flow.

(Left) You can block off a bubblevator bottom entryway with signs. (Right) Create a platform to step on and off of.

CHAPTER 7
STEP BY STEP GUARDIAN FARM

eyond tapping, collecting, building, and adventuring, you can greatly improve your experience and add to your loot by hunting down challenges to complete, completing your journal, and using boosts to help you in adventures and more.

The key element in deciding how to build a guardian farm (or any mob farm) are the rules for guardian spawning.

1. Use the rules of mob spawning to create an area where only that mob spawns.

2. Move the mobs as quickly as possible into a smaller area where you can kill them or they can be killed automatically.

Guardian spawning rules include:

• Guardians spawn in water blocks only in the area of the ocean monument. (They specifically need two vertical water blocks and a third transparent block above these two. The third transparent block can be another block of water, or a sign, or air, etc.)

• They spawn much more often in water that has a ceiling over it (no exposure to the sky).

• The ocean monument spawning area is 58 wide by 58 deep by 24 block high area, whose bottom aligns with the floor level of the monument. This is usually at y=39, with the top of the spawning area usually at y=61.

Other relevant mob spawning rules include:

- Hostile mobs spawn within 128 blocks of the player.

- Hostile mobs won't spawn within 24 blocks of the player.

- Many guardian farms remove the entire ocean monument, and wall off the huge spawnable area and drain it (a "monumental" effort, but pretty straightforward).

Then, inside the empty spawning area, you can create a smaller, enclosed, waterfilled space that guardians will now spawn in. The guardians are next moved, by water flow, into a smaller space where they can be killed automatically or by a player with a sword. The reason for creating the smaller spawning space is to avoid having to move spawned guardians over a long distance to the killing area.

Another tactic is to not worry about getting the maximum spawns possible from the ocean monument area, and build a smaller farm above the monument, without draining the full spawning space. You can use soul sand to push guardians up into a upper collection area. There, the guardians are forced by water streams into a central, blocked off column where they fall, landing on top of campfires.

Some of the key Minecraft mechanics involved in creating this farms include:

• Soul sand in water will push mobs vertically above it up to the surface.

• You can push mobs horizontally with water flow.

• Water flows for 8 blocks before stopping.

• Multiple, side-by-side, open fence gates will allow mobs to pass through them, but not water.

• Guardians (and other mobs) will die on top of campfires.

• You can gather drops that fall from killed mobs using hoppers below campfires that link to chests.

Versions of this smaller farm push the guardians on the surface into a handful of large nether portals. Because the nether portals are so close, they send the guardians all to a single portal in the nether, where they fall into a smaller space where they can be killed.

You can watch videos of easy to build guardian farms on Youtube from Minecrafters Cortezerino, Voltrox, Avomance, and Wattles.

To make a very simple, no-drain guardian farm, based on these farms, do the following:

1. Drain the top room of an ocean monument.

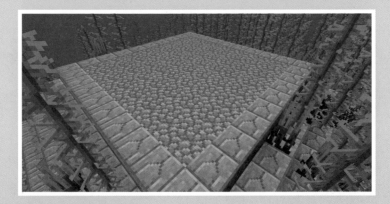

2. Remove the top arches on this top room so that the roof is flat.

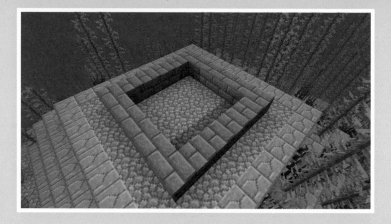

3. Build a 6x6 block square empty column centered on top of the monument.

4. Build this up to just one block below the surface. These walls surround the 4x4 space the guardians fall into.

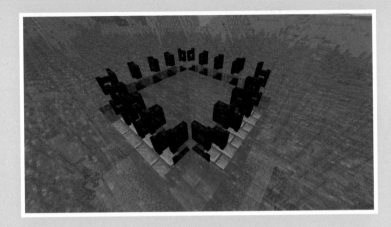

5. Place a 2 high row of 4 opened fence gates per row on top of the center of each wall of the column. The top row of these gates will be just above the ocean's surface.

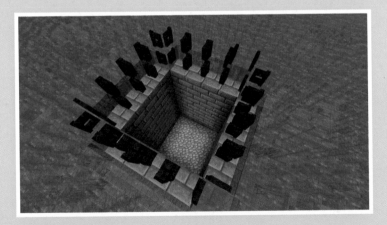

6. Drain the inside of the column.

7. Continue building the column down and inside the monument, to the floor of the top room, breaking the roof blocks that fall inside the column. I've used glass blocks here, and flattened out the floor of the top room.

8. At the bottom of the column, place a double chest outside of the column.

9. Inside the column, link eighteen hoppers (sixteen inside the column and two to link these to the double chest) so that they will push items into the double chest. (Break and replace blocks as you need to get in and out!)

10. Above the hoppers place 16 campfires.

11. Back at the top of the column, build a temporary platform of dirt on top of the water's surface. It should extend 8 blocks out from the top fence gates on each side. (The orange and yellow wool blocks here are only to show the length of one side of the square.) If there is kelp growing beneath this area, remove it, as kelp growing to the surface can interfere with water source blocks.

12. Place six corner blocks as shown at each corner.

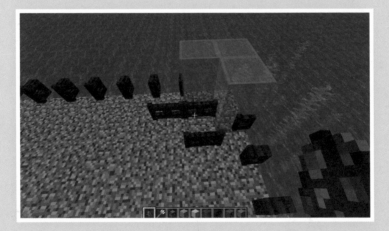

13. Between each set of corner blocks place a row of opened fence gates.

14. Place three fence gates at each corner as shown (A) and then open them (B).

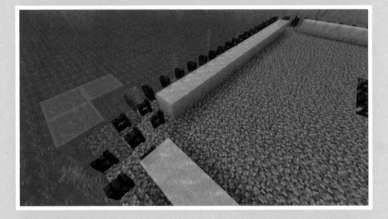

15. Along each side, in front of each opened fence gate, place water blocks. Here, I've placed ice blocks to show where these go. (If you have them, ice blocks are a great way to place water source blocks – once they're placed, just use a pick axe to turn them into water.)

16. At each corner, place a single water block on top of the top corner fence gate. Again, an ice block here shows where the water source block is placed at each corner.

17. The water should flow from each side to the central column without going into the column. (If you are using ice blocks, now is the time to break them (along the sides first) so that they turn into water source blocks.

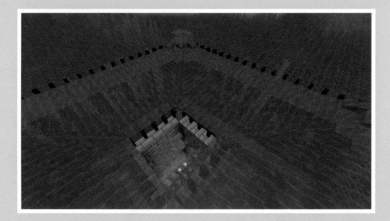

18. Remove all the dirt blocks.

19. Underneath the top collection area (bordered by the larger square of fence gates) – and no further out-- place soul sand on top of the ocean monument's roofs. You'll need to flatten some of the roofs and remove any kelp or sea grass in the way. Be careful, as it is pretty easy to get pushed yourself into the bubble column. Don't forget to build an entrance into the top room, as well! You can use signs to stop water from entering.

This farm should net you a steady stream of prismarine shards, prismarine crystal, cod, and the occasional stray ink sac. If you want to up the drops, build an AFK (away from keyboard) platform 128 blocks above the bottom of the spawning area. This should limit other types of mobs spawning outside of the ocean monument area and increase drops.